SCHIRMER'S LIBRARY
OF MUSICAL CLASSICS

Vol. 1988

ANTONÍN DVOŘÁK

Romance
Op. 11

For Violin and Piano

ISBN 978-0-7935-5747-9

G. SCHIRMER, Inc.

DISTRIBUTED BY

HAL•LEONARD®
CORPORATION
7777 W. BLUEMOUND RD. P.O. BOX 13819 MILWAUKEE, WI 53213

FOREWORD

Antonín Dvořák's composition *Romance, op. 11* exists in two versions: for violin and piano and for violin and small orchestra. After analyzing quite a few details, Otakar Šourek, the well-known Dvořák scholar, came to the conclusion that the orchestral score of the composition was written after the version with piano.

Both autographs are without a date, so it is impossible to ascertain otherwise when they were written. The opus number, as we know from other examples, is not necessarily a reliable guide. We do know the date of the first performance: December 9, 1877.

The present edition is based on the version "Kritické vydání podle skladatelova rukopisu" (Critical edition after the composer's manuscript, published by the Antonín Dvořák Society in 1955 in Prague).

The information presented in the score reflects the composer's original version, with the exception of some added dynamics which are enclosed in brackets. The separate violin part has been altered by the editor.

—R.K.

ROMANCE

Violin part edited by Rok Klopčič

Antonín Dvořák, op. 11

Andante con moto ♪.= 132

*) ossia:

ROMANCE

VIOLIN SOLO

Violin part edited by Rok Klopčič

Antonín Dvořák, op. 11

Andante con moto ♪ = 132

2